HAL•LEONARD
INSTRUMENTAL
PLAY-ALONG

AUDIO
ACCESS
INCLUDED

PLAYBACK+
Speed • Pitch • Balance • Loop

# TRUMPET

# CHRISTMAS CLASSICS

Audio arrangements by Peter Deneff

To access audio visit:
**www.halleonard.com/mylibrary**

Enter Code
**1022-7542-7605-8369**

ISBN 978-1-4950-7058-7

HAL•LEONARD®
CORPORATION
7777 W. BLUEMOUND RD. P.O. BOX 13819 MILWAUKEE, WI 53213

In Australia Contact:
**Hal Leonard Australia Pty. Ltd.**
4 Lentara Court
Cheltenham, Victoria, 3192 Australia
Email: ausadmin@halleonard.com.au

Visit Hal Leonard Online at
**www.halleonard.com**

# ANGELS WE HAVE HEARD ON HIGH

TRUMPET

Traditional French Carol

# BRING A TORCH, JEANNETTE, ISABELLA

TRUMPET

17th Century French Provençal Carol

# COVENTRY CAROL

TRUMPET

Traditional English Melody

# FUM, FUM, FUM

TRUMPET

Traditional Catalonian Carol

# GO, TELL IT ON THE MOUNTAIN

TRUMPET

African-American Spiritual

# GOD REST YE MERRY, GENTLEMEN

TRUMPET

Traditional English Carol

# HERE WE COME A-CAROLING

TRUMPET

Traditional

# THE HOLLY AND THE IVY

TRUMPET

18th Century English Carol

# I SAW THREE SHIPS

TRUMPET

Traditional English Carol

# JINGLE BELLS

TRUMPET

Words and Music by
J. PIERPONT

# O COME, ALL YE FAITHFUL

TRUMPET

Music by JOHN FRANCIS WADE

# O HOLY NIGHT

TRUMPET

French Words by PLACIDE CAPPEAU
English Words by JOHN S. DWIGHT
Music by ADOLPHE ADAM

# SILENT NIGHT

TRUMPET

Words by JOSEPH MOHR
Music by FRANZ X. GRUBER

# STILL, STILL, STILL

TRUMPET

Salzburg Melody, c.1819

# WHAT CHILD IS THIS?

TRUMPET

16th Century English Melody